Like a Pro

Karate

Yolanda Ridge

AV2
www.openlightbox.com

1-Year K–5 Subscription
ISBN 978-1-7911-3320-7

Like a Pro

Karate

Contents

I love karate.
I am going to do karate today.

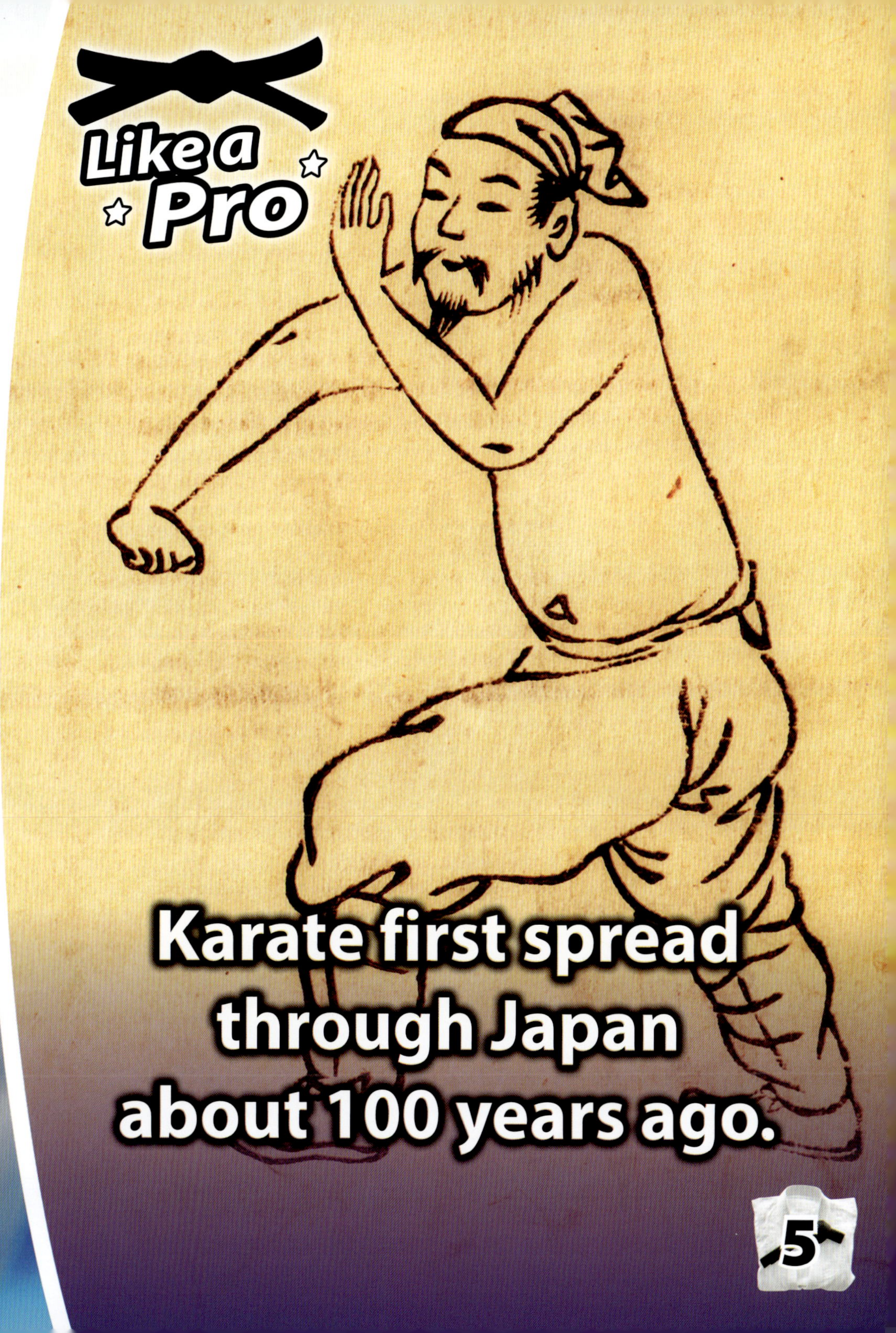

Karate first spread through Japan about 100 years ago.

I wear white pants and a white jacket to practice karate.

Like a Pro

The uniform worn to practice karate is called a gi.

Karate belts come in different colors. Beginners wear white belts.

Like a Pro

A karate expert wears a black belt.

I go to a building called a dojo for karate class.

Like a Pro

The word *dojo* means "a place of the way."

Before I practice karate,
I do stretches to warm up.

Like a Pro

Karate masters must be flexible and strong.

My teammates and I line up at the start of karate practice.

Like a Pro

It is important for karate students to respect their teacher. Bowing is one way to show respect.

I strike the air using my hand, elbow, knee, and foot.

Like a Pro

Strikes can be tested by hitting dummies or boards.

I spar against other students. I earn points for successful strikes.

Like a Pro

The Karate World Championships take place every two years.

I love karate.

KARATE FACTS

These pages provide more detail about interesting facts found in the book. They are intended to be used by adults as a learning support to help young readers round out their knowledge of each sport featured in the *Like a Pro* series.

Pages 4–5

Getting Ready Karate is a martial art that involves kicking, striking, and defensive blocking. Concentration and respect are important in karate, which is focused on self-defense. The sport started in what is now Okinawa, a group of islands in southern Japan. It developed over several centuries before being introduced to mainland Japan in the 1920s.

Pages 6–7

What I Wear *Gi* is the Japanese word for clothing. A karate gi is made of light cloth that allows mobility. The gi is also referred to as a *karategi*, *keikogi*, or *dogi*. If someone's gi is not clean, they may not be able to participate in class or competition. The pants are called *zuban*, while the robe or jacket is an *uwagai*.

Pages 8–9

What I Use A belt, or *obi*, is the third part of a karate gi. Its color signifies rank. Different schools of karate have different belt colors that may include yellow, green, blue, purple, brown, or black. A beginner generally wears a white belt. A 10th-degree black belt is the highest possible rank. Degrees are indicated by a white stripe, or *dan*.

Pages 10–11

Where I Play A dojo is a school or hall where people learn and practice martial arts. There are very strict rules of etiquette in a karate dojo. One example is doing a standing bow when entering or exiting the dojo. It is a place of respect, discipline, structure, and self-control.

Pages 12–13

Warming Up Karate involves quick actions that snap the joints, so it is important to warm up properly. Dynamic stretching, in which joints and muscles are stretched through movement rather than static holds, is recommended. Twisting movements and activation of core muscles also help improve mobility.

Pages 14–15

Team Play At the beginning of karate practice, the instructor orders everyone to line up. Students stand shoulder to shoulder in order of rank or height. Everyone moves through the forms together. It is very important to respect the instructor, other participants, and the dojo by bowing, obeying instructions, and following rules.

Pages 16–17

Playing the Game Most karate classes practice *kata*, a sequence of movements or forms. Kata are taught in stages and repeated to improve punches, kicks, blocks, footwork, and breathing techniques. Karate practitioners can achieve higher ranks by doing individual kata performances that are ranked by judges.

Pages 18–19

Winning the Game In karate competitions, opponents are matched by rank and size. Points are gained by throws, as well as punches and kicks that strike different parts of the body. Referees determine how many points are awarded based on elements including technique, form, timing, awareness, and attitude. The person with the most points wins.

Pages 20–21

I Love Karate Karate is a way to focus both mind and body while learning self-discipline and socialization skills. Karate is written with Japanese characters that mean "empty hand." It evolved as a way of defending against enemies without the use of weapons. At its heart, karate is a martial art dedicated to respect and peace.

KEY WORDS

Research has shown that as much as 65 percent of all written material published in English is made up of 300 words. These 300 words cannot be taught using pictures or learned by sounding them out. They must be recognized by sight. This book contains 47 common sight words to help young readers improve their reading fluency and comprehension. This book also teaches young readers several important content words, such as proper nouns. These words are paired with pictures to aid in learning and improve understanding.

Page	Sight Words First Appearance
4	am, do, I, to
5	a, about, first, like, through, years
6	and, white
7	is, the
8	come, different, in
10	for, go
11	means, of, place, way, word
12	before, up
13	be, must
14	at, line, my, start
15	important, it, one, show, their
16	air, hand
17	by, can, or
18	other, points
19	every, take, two

Page	Content Words First Appearance
4	karate
5	Japan
6	jacket, pants
7	gi, uniform
8	beginners, belts, colors
9	expert
10	building, class, dojo
12	stretches
13	masters
14	teammates
15	respect, students, teacher
16	foot, elbow, knee
17	boards, dummies, strikes
19	Karate World Championships

Published by Lightbox Learning Inc.
276 5th Avenue, Suite 704 #917
New York, NY 10001
Website: www.openlightbox.com

Library of Congress Control Number: 2023935736

ISBN 978-1-7911-5793-7 (hardcover)
ISBN 978-1-7911-5794-4 (softcover)
ISBN 978-1-7911-5795-1 (multi-user eBook)

042023
100922

Printed in Guangzhou, China
1 2 3 4 5 6 7 8 9 0 27 26 25 24 23

Project Coordinator: John Willis
Designer: Ana María Vidal

Every reasonable effort has been made to trace ownership and to obtain permission to reprint copyright material. The publisher would be pleased to have any errors or omissions brought to its attention so that they may be corrected in subsequent printings.

The publisher acknowledges Alamy, Getty Images, and Shutterstock as its primary image suppliers for this title.